For Huang Luo Yi
—A. R.

Carolrhoda Books
A division of Lerner Publishing Group, Inc.
241 First Avenue North
Minneapolis, MN 55401 U.S.A.

Website address: www.lernerbooks.com

Main body text set in ITC Benguiat Gothic Std Medium 14.5/20. Typeface provided by Adobe Systems.

Library of Congress Cataloging-in-Publication Data

Rockwell, Anne F.
    Hey, Charleston! : the true story of the Jenkins Orphanage Band / by Anne Rockwell ; illustrated by Colin Bootman.
       p.   cm.
    ISBN 978-0-7613-5565-6 (lib. bdg. : alk. paper)
    ISBN 978-0-7613-8843-2 (eBook)
    1. Jenkins Orphanage Band—Juvenile literature. 2. African American musicians—South Carolina—Charleston—Juvenile literature. I. Bootman, Colin, ill. II. Title.
    ML28.C35J469 2013
    784.4'4060757915—dc22   2010001525

Manufactured in the United States of America
1 – DP – 7/15/13

Hey, Charleston!

The True Story of the Jenkins Orphanage Band

JENKINS Orphanage BAND
20 FDA

Anne Rockwell

Illustrations by Colin Bootman

Carolrhoda Books Minneapolis

Have you ever known someone who was always trying to turn bad into good, always seeing hope where others saw despair? Then you know the kind of person the Reverend Daniel Joseph Jenkins was.

He was the pastor of a small church in Charleston, South Carolina. Even with his preacher's salary, he still needed extra money to make ends meet. So he also delivered scrap wood to people who used it to keep their houses warm. On a cold night more than a hundred years ago, he was collecting wood that had fallen from freight trains when he heard moaning and sobbing coming from somewhere. He found a group of little boys huddled together near the tracks. Their stomachs hurt from hunger, and their teeth were chattering from the cold. They were orphans with no home. Reverend Jenkins took them to his church. He gave them hot soup and warm blankets and a place to sleep, even if it was only a narrow pew or the floor of the church. He knew how it felt to be an orphan, for he'd been one too.

Soon more orphans came knocking at the church door. They'd heard they were welcome there. The good people of Reverend Jenkins's church did all they could, but eventually they ran out of room and food and clothes and everything a big family of growing children needs.

Now, Reverend Jenkins was not only kind and hardworking. He was also a most impressive person. He was six feet seven inches tall and very handsome. He had a wonderful speaking voice and gracious manners that moved whoever heard him preach. So when he went before the city officials, drew himself up to his full height, and asked in his fine preacher's voice if he might have an abandoned warehouse for his orphanage, the officials not only gave him the warehouse—they gave him a hundred dollars besides.

A hundred dollars could buy a lot more in the early 1900s than today, but all the same, the money soon ran out with so many children to feed.

The warehouse was better than nothing, but it was also a mighty noisy place. You see a prison was next door, and the inmates were always banging on windows and walls and shouting swear words that Reverend Jenkins would rather his orphans didn't learn. But as usual, he figured out how to turn bad into good. He led the orphans in singing praise to the Lord above until they drowned out the shouting, the banging, and the clanging. Those orphans were fine singers. And their singing gave him an idea.

When the Reverend Daniel Jenkins
was a boy, he'd been a slave as well as
an orphan. He was a baby in the 1860s
during the great Civil War, a war that
freed all the slaves in the United States,
including him. People in Charleston still
spoke of the fighting and dying and also
of soldiers, some dressed in blue, some
dressed in gray, all marching to battle to
the sound of marching-band music. Reverend
Jenkins figured that maybe the instruments were
somewhere in attics or cellars. So he sent the word
throughout Charleston that he'd be glad to take any
old band instruments off people's hands.

And there sure were plenty! Cornets, tenor horns, saxhorns, baritones, and tubas, along with big drums and tiny piccolos, began turning up at the door of the orphanage. Sure, they were dented and banged up from rifle and cannon fire, but Reverend Jenkins, who was always looking for a way to turn bad into good, set everyone to work polishing up those horns and drums until they shone like the sun.

He hired the best teachers he could find to teach the orphans to read music and to play those instruments. He thought the orphans could bring joy to the streets of Charleston. Wouldn't people pay good money to have a little joy? Reverend Jenkins was sure this was so. With the money, he planned to buy a farm where the orphans could grow all the food they needed, year in and year out. He wanted them to grow up to be strong, good people who could provide for themselves.

Before long, the Jenkins Orphanage Band
was playing marches on street corners.
But the music probably sounded a little
different than it had all those years
ago during the Civil War. Lots of the
orphans were descended from
the Geechee or Gullah
people who lived on
the islands around
Charleston.

These people hadn't changed a lot since their enslaved ancestors came from Africa, and they had their own way of making music, their own kind of rhythm. They called this kind of music "rag." So whenever someone in the audience shouted, **"Give us some rag!"** the kids knew just what to do.

They'd start playing the old band songs African-style. A couple of Geechee boys would lead the band by doing a dance—twisting and twirling and tapping their toes, knocking their knees, and flapping their arms. As they danced, the musicians played the marches with plenty of rag. It didn't matter that their instruments were banged up by bullets and cannons. In the old days in Africa, musicians hung seashells from their horns to give their music that raggedy, rattly sound that those beat-up instruments already had.

But the band still didn't collect a lot of money. Most people in Charleston didn't have much more money than the band members. Reverend Jenkins decided they should go north to New York City, where he thought the band could make more money. His idea worked! When the people in New York heard the band, they loved the raggedy music best of all and would shout **"Hey, Charleston!"**—for they only knew the boys in the band came from Charleston—**"Give us some rag!"**

It didn't take long for the pretty ladies and the slick gentlemen of New York started imitating those Geechee boys, with their twisting, twirling, tapping toes; their knocking knees, bent elbows, and flapping arms. People called the dance the Charleston. Before you knew it, everyone was doing that dance.

Reverend Jenkins was able
to move the orphans—and he had
about five hundred of them by now—
to a new house. They learned regular
school subjects as well as music. They
also learned trades so they could earn
a living when it was time for them to
leave the orphanage. But music was
the main thing. The music teaching was
so good that pretty soon mothers and
fathers asked to pay to send their
children to study music
with the orphans.

The band kept traveling. The Jenkins Orphanage Band became so popular that they were invited to march in the inaugural parade for U.S. president Theodore Roosevelt. The money they made allowed the orphanage to finally buy its farm outside Charleston.

In 1914 five bands were invited to play before Britain's king George V at the Anglo-American Exposition in London, England. The Jenkins Orphanage Band was one of them. They crossed the Atlantic Ocean by ship and in London found elegant new uniforms waiting for them. The band performed for raucous crowds, earning the orphanage more money. But as Reverend Jenkins knew, just as bad could turn into good, the opposite could also happen. And it did.

In August of 1914, Germany invaded Belgium. In support of Belgium, Britain declared war on Germany. World War I had begun. Since the British government had invited the band to London, it made sure that the band members had rooms on a ship that would take them back home to peace and safety.

But other Americans in Britain weren't so lucky. Their money was frozen in British banks until the end of the war. And who knew when that would be? They were stranded and frightened.

One American in this predicament was a well-to-do man Reverend Jenkins had known in Charleston. When Reverend Jenkins heard about this man's plight, he remembered how the man and other leaders of the city had given him a hundred dollars for his orphans. The Reverend didn't think any good deed should go unthanked. So he offered to lend the man money for him and his family to get home.

Plenty of others needed help too. Reverend Jenkins counted up
the money the band had made in London. He saw he had enough
to buy tickets for each of those stranded Americans. So he did.

The ship sailed from London without any fanfare, sneaking silently through the cold, dark waters of the Atlantic Ocean to escape the German boats that might try to sink it. But as soon as the ship reached American waters and safety, someone aboard called out, "Hey, Charleston! Give us some rag!"

You can be sure that the band began to play good and loud. The Geechee boys led it— toes twisting, twirling, and tapping; knees knocking; and arms flapping. They'd never played better. And everyone joined in the dance—passengers, sailors, the captain, and the cook.

When the ship sailed into New York Harbor, crowds were waiting to greet them. Flags were flying, and people were dancing on the dock as the Jenkins Orphanage Band marched down the gangplank, playing tubas and trombones, saxhorns and cornets, and sousaphones and drums.

Those kids were mighty tired when they returned to their farm. Everyone there was full of joy to see them safely home. As they lay down to sleep that night, those band players knew they had done what Reverend Jenkins always taught them. They had turned bad into good.

AUTHOR'S NOTE ON THE JENKINS ORPHANAGE BAND

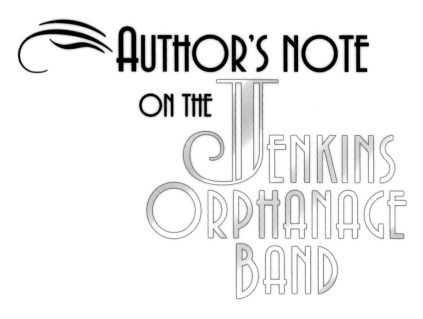

Jazz blends musical traditions from Africa with those of Europe. This is a fact often acknowledged. But where and when did that blending happen? Who had the inspiration that launched the great American art form? There are many answers to this question, but the story of the Jenkins Orphanage Band is one of the best, and the history of a good man and the children he helped deserves to be better known.

During slavery, different peoples from West Africa brought their own music to North America. The Gullah people of South Carolina came largely from Senegal, and they called their style of music "rag." The style's syncopated rhythms and give-and-take among instruments come directly from the African musical tradition, and they paired well with the American military band instruments that the Reverend Jenkins was able to put in the hands of quite a few Gullah children. And so the blending began.

The Jenkins Orphanage took in boys from about six years old, and each learned how to play all the band's instruments. By the age of seventeen, most graduated equipped with an education to get by in the world. And many did quite a bit more than get by.

Musicians who became famous around the globe in their own right told of their experiences and the demanding training at the Jenkins Orphanage. The American big band sound has roots in the Jenkins Orphanage Band through musicians like Cat Anderson and Jabbo Smith, both trumpeters with Duke Ellington, and Freddie Green, a guitarist for Count Basie's Orchestra. Each of these musicians got training at the orphanage. When the United States entered World War I in 1917, one of the teachers from the band joined the all-black Harlem Hellfighters regiment and played in its acclaimed band, started by pioneering African American bandleader James Reese Europe. The Hellfighters band brought the Jenkins sound to Paris, where it found a lasting and loving home.

Reverend Jenkins's success was imitated in New Orleans; in 1914 that city organized its own Colored Waif's Home Brass Band. A young trumpeter in that band grew up to become the great Louis Armstrong.

Daniel Joseph Jenkins's legacy lives on not only in music but also in the Jenkins Institute for Children outside Charleston. This is a place where children of all races and ethnic origins in need of help can get support and protection. And this is just what Reverend Jenkins would have wished.

Selected Bibliography

Chilton, John. *A Jazz Nursery: The Story of the Jenkins Orphanage Band.*
    London: Bloomsbury Book Shop, 1980.

Rosen, Robert. *A Short History of Charleston.* Charleston: University of
    South Carolina Press, 1997.

Shirley, Wayne D. "The Jenkins Orphanage Band and *Porgy and Bess.*" In
    Music, American Made: Essays in Honor of John Graziano, edited by
    John Koegel. Sterling Heights, MI: Harmonie Park Press, 2011.